THE
FESTIVAL
BOOK

THE FESTIVAL BOOK

Michael Odell

BANTAM PRESS

LONDON · NEW YORK · TORONTO · SYDNEY · AUCKLAND

TRANSWORLD PUBLISHERS
61–63 Uxbridge Road, London W5 5SA
www.penguin.co.uk

Transworld is part of the Penguin Random House group of companies
whose addresses can be found at global.penguinrandomhouse.com

 Penguin
Random House
UK

First published in Great Britain in 2017 by Bantam Press
an imprint of Transworld Publishers

A CIP catalogue record for this book
is available from the British Library.

ISBN 9780593078716

CONTENTS

For Rosa

See you in the 21 Pilots mosh pit

A SHORT HISTORY OF FESTIVALS

FARMERS PLAY a crucial role in the history of rock festivals. Although other festivals pre-date it, America's legendary Woodstock is considered the granddaddy of them all and first took place on a dairy farm in Bethel, New York state in August 1969. Owner of the farm, Max Yasgur, stepped in after other local venues pulled out, and was paid £30,000 in compensation for lost productivity. However, his neighbours weren't keen. They put up signs reading:

STOP MAX'S HIPPIE MUSIC FESTIVAL.

NO 150,000 HIPPIES HERE.

BUY NO MILK.

But rock fans didn't listen. On the day, local police reported 1.5 million people were headed for Woodstock, even though organizers hadn't finished erecting ticket booths or security fences. As a result, the organizers decided at the last minute to make it a free event. Attendance estimates vary between 500,000 and 1 million, and farmer Yasgur gave them all complimentary water and milk.

'We older guys need to do more to close the generation gap and understand young people,' he said. Woodstock established the idea of boozy, carefree camping near the sound of rock music for future generations. Woodstock was the moment that rock festivals came of age.

In the UK, the inaugural Isle of Wight Festival occurred just eleven days after the first Woodstock, and managed to attract Bob Dylan as a headline act. He had been expected to perform at Woodstock (which was pretty much held in his back yard) but he was already en route to Britain.

A year later, Michael Eavis started the Pilton Pop, Folk & Blues Festival on his Somerset dairy farm. Entry was £1 and included all the milk you could drink. Fifteen hundred people attended. The Kinks were booked but cancelled and T. Rex stepped in. Eavis had to pay T. Rex out of his 'milk money' and lost £500 putting on the show.

'I hadn't been with my second wife very long and we wanted to make new friends, so it was a way of being friendly and letting the neighbours know what we were like,' he said.

The next year, Eavis left the festival in the hands of two upper-crust hippies: Arabella Churchill, the granddaughter of wartime prime minister Winston Churchill, and Andrew Kerr, a man who sold his father's collection of antique shotguns to fund the event. They changed the festival's name to the Glastonbury Fair.

WOODSTOCK 196

GLASTONBURY 1971

THE CROWD BEAM PURE LOVE AT YOU AND IT TRAVELS THROUGH MY GUITAR AND I BEAM IT RIGHT BACK, MAN.

JIMI HENDRIX AT WOODSTOCK

In the 1980s rock festivals struggled. Punk, new wave and indie music didn't produce any notable festival-friendly acts to succeed the 70s rock giants. Also the age of MTV and video encouraged pure pop and no one was seriously going to watch cheesy 80s megastars Wham! or Duran Duran in a field. Instead it was dance music that led the way with unofficial festivals or 'raves'.

In the 90s Britpop helped revive UK festivals by producing bands like Blur and Oasis whom people wanted to see play live. TV also played its part raising the profile of festivals. In 1994, Channel 4 started broadcasting Glastonbury for the first time (a largely unknown Oasis played after lunch on the Other Stage) and a vast new audience became curious about muddy tents and moshpits.

The internet all but destroyed the music industry in the noughties by making recorded music 'free'. Nevertheless a new generation wanted to enjoy the communal experience of a rock festival and bands were happy to make their living playing live.

As the big festivals became harder to access, smaller boutique festivals emerged which could serve a smaller and more discerning audience. Gatherings like Bestival, Latitude and Green Man don't just offer live bands but adventurous food, performing arts, fancy dress and a complete alternative lifestyle.

Glastonbury's Michael Eavis says: 'It seems incredible that nearly fifty years after we did that first one, festivals have become a really important part of British culture.' He can say that again. There are over 200 music festivals each summer and Eavis now has 177,000 'friends' turning up at his farm every year.

FESTIVAL
TRIBES

THE ICONIC ONE:
GLASTONBURY

Glastonbury embodies the spirit of British festivals best, mainly because it is still organized by an idealistic farmer and his daughter. 'Glastonbury is special because it is a place full of non-conformists and free-thinkers,' Michael Eavis told the BBC in 2016. 'This is the home of mavericks.' Eavis and his daughter Emily have established a non-profit-making jamboree with an identifiable creed: come and freak out on our farm while helping out the poor and the environment.

Glastonbury is expensive but you get 2,200 performances and it does raise a lot of money for charity. The extra-curricular stuff is the wackiest and most thought-provoking around (for example, a women-only tent where you can learn DIY, the notorious under-ground bar called the Rabbit Hole and the fantastic LGBT club NYC Downlow).

People grumble that the festival lost its 'soul' when the 15-foot super-fence went up in 2002, and then again when photo ID was introduced in 2007. But because it takes place in the Vale of Avalon, a part of Somerset deemed the most sacred site in Britain by assorted fairies, wizards and shamans, it does still feel very special.

THE ONE TO SEE LEGENDS:
THE ISLE OF WIGHT

The Isle of Wight Festival has some impressive history. Bob Dylan performed there in 1969 (watched by a crowd that included John Lennon, Keith Richards, Eric Clapton, Liz Taylor and Richard Burton) and in 1970 between 300,000 and 600,000 people enjoyed a line-up that included The Doors, The Who, Joni Mitchell, Leonard Cohen and Jimi Hendrix (who died just three weeks after his performance). Entry was £3.

The festival was banned but then revived in 2002 and has since managed to attract some major legends, including Bruce Springsteen, Fleetwood Mac, the Rolling Stones, David Bowie, Paul McCartney, Neil Young and The Police.

THE ONE FOR
SELF-IMPROVEMENT: LATITUDE

Everyone expects to come home from a festival with a henna tattoo, a tummy bug, maybe even nits. But a qualification? At Latitude you can do an Arts Council-backed Arts Award. There are also talks from authors and drama classes. Expect wicker hampers, posh toilet paper and well-educated folk drinking good rosé.

It's in Norfolk, which is hard to get to, and it's a bit like a giggly, middle-class barbecue that has got slightly out of control. The setting is great and the boutique feel is perfect if you don't like the crush of a massive festival. Good acts, too.

THE GAP-YEAR FESTIVAL:
WOMAD

You used to think Foo Fighters were edgy. Then you took a gap year and discovered that there is more out there than Western pop. There is nose-flute music and Japanese choral with drums. WOMAD is where you can relive your gap-year experiences. Expect interesting late-night cultural conversations with a Thai monk who plays a yak's horn, and lots of fancy foreign food.

WOMAD has a very different feel to the enormous festivals like Glasto, with 'only' 40,000 people. It feels cosy and friendly and the music is stuff you're not going to encounter anywhere else.

THE ONE TO WEAR LEATHER AT:
DOWNLOAD

Some music festivals have gone off topic. They've become about food or dressing-up, with a bit of music thrown in. But Download is a proper rock festival. There's heavy metal and death metal and tech metal and ska-metal. Plus amazing staging and lighting. Not for everyone but what it does, it does brilliantly.

It's held at Donington Park in Leicester and back in the day it used to be called Monsters of Rock. Black Sabbath, Iron Maiden, all the heavy legends have played there. Have you got a belt with a big buckle, and black biker boots? You'll need them.

DOWNLOAD 2016

THE OLD-SCHOOL FESTIVAL:
READING & LEEDS

Reading claims to be the UK's oldest festival, although it started out as the National Jazz Festival held in Richmond, south-west London and then moved to Plumpton village in Sussex. Anyhow, it has been in Reading since 1971, Leeds since 1999 and has prided itself on not becoming too fancy like some of the others. Before festivals got eco-minded and family-friendly, they were little more than First World War battle re-enactments with some loud music in the mix. And Reading & Leeds Festival pretty much still is that. It happens after GCSE exam results come out. All that hatred against the education system unleashed in one field? Awesome.

This is the best festival for audience participation. If you don't like an artist, then you're encouraged to vent your displeasure. Airborne plastic bottles filled with wee are not uncommon. Less pop and more rock than Glasto, it has fewer hippies and more raucous fun.

TOP FIVE QUICKEST EXITS FROM READING

1   In 2004, Finnish rock band The Rasmus abandoned their performance after bass player Eero Heinonen was hit in the face by a clump of mud and required medical treatment. They had been forced off stage by bottles and mud after completing just one song, 'First Day Of My Life'.

2   In 1999, former Dexys Midnight Runners frontman Kevin Rowland appeared on stage in a white mini-dress and stockings. His gender-fluid performance was subdued by airborne missiles after 5 minutes.

3   In 1983, reggae band Steel Pulse were bottled off stage after 10 minutes. Singer David Hinds noted afterwards: 'I thought rock fans were supposed to be open-minded.'

4   In the same year, American rapper 50 Cent was negatively reviewed in a hail of glassware after 18 minutes. Uniquely, he attempted to fight back, throwing his mic at the crowd.

5   In 1988, Meatloaf took the hint from a hail of receptacles after 20 minutes. Afterwards, the American rocker said, 'There were bottles and cans but I also saw some food out there. That is ridiculous to waste so much food when people are starving.'

THE PSYCHEDELIC FOLK ONE: GREEN MAN

Green Man takes place in the wilds of Wales' Brecon Beacons and the Mountain Stage has a reputation as a majestic natural amphitheatre. It has a free and pagan feel, with camping opportunities available long before the music begins. There is wild swimming (no, not waving your arms frantically because you never quite mastered the front crawl, but devil-may-care, often nude bathing in nearby rivers and lakes), forest walking and foraging, plus pony-trekking in the beautiful surroundings for a whole week beforehand. You won't get big names here but always interesting and eclectic acts.

If you stay till the end, on Sunday night they burn the massive green man effigy.

THE ONE FOR ECO-WARRIORS: SHAMBALA

Shambala happens in Northamptonshire and one of the first things you will notice when you get on-site is that your brain doesn't ache like it does at some big festivals. Why? Because no one is trying to sell you anything. It is ad- and marketing-free. Shambala director Chris Johnson says, 'We're tapping in to something which has perhaps been lost in our Western society: the need for celebration and connection on a deep level without passive consumerist messages and corporate agendas.'

Blimey! Sounds a little serious and po-faced but actually, at Shambala, festival-goers are encouraged to create the 'vibe' themselves and, in recent years, there have been roaming theatrical productions, shadow dancing, trampolining and a late-night samba procession. What's more, its sustainable credentials are really something. Its vegetable-oil-fuelled generator has won awards. Recently, they went meat- and fish-free and introduced an Insect Bar.

The Insect Bar does a reasonable trade in 'triple bug chilli' and 'eggybuggybread'. Now, that may sound disgusting or wacky but apparently, insects are the sustainable, protein-rich way forward. Shambala is great fun but it also makes you think about the world and offers a window on alternative lifestyles.

THE ONE FOR RUMBLING TUMMIES: **WILDERNESS**

Wilderness Festival has music but all anyone ever talks about is the food. It's incredible. And if people aren't eating, then they're giving talks about it. There are chefs everywhere and you half expect Gordon Ramsay or Nigella to be headlining the main stage with a whisk.

Frankly, this is a posh festival. As well as the grub, there are philosophy sessions, a champagne bar and lessons in how to mix cocktails. Reading it ain't.

FESTIVALS ARE FULL
OF RAIN AND MUD
AND SHIT AND
I DON'T KNOW
WHY ANYONE
WOULD CHOOSE
TO PUT THEMSELVES
THROUGH THAT.
UNLESS YOU'RE
PLAYING.

LIAM GALLAGHER

THE ONE TO SEE CELEBS:
V FESTIVAL

Cynics say V is the festival you go to if you don't really like festivals. Basically, it's all about the celebs. If they've had a few radio hits, they're on the bill. And yes, they do attract some amazing names.

V Festival has a *very* corporate reputation. So go if you really want to get your fix of superstars but don't expect people to listen to stories about your mind-bending, soul-cleansing, alternative festival experience when you get home.

RIHANNA 2016

THE ONE TO SHOW OFF COOL TRAINERS: **WIRELESS**

Wireless is full of cool people in gleaming trainers and it has the best dance and R&B acts. But there are no real 'extras'. Where's the pig-racing or the fire-eating? There isn't any!

Wireless Festival happens in London's Finsbury Park and there's no camping.

THE ONE IN SCOTLAND:
T IN THE PARK

T in the Park is held in one of the most beautiful places for a rock concert ever. It was moved to the grounds of Strathallan Castle in 2015, after someone pointed out there was a BP oil pipeline running underneath its previous location of eighteen years, Balado airfield. Verdict? A few issues with transport on narrow country lanes but otherwise it has been a good move. The thing is, Scottish rock fans are just a bit more up for it than their spoilt southern neighbours.

THE A-LIST ONE: **COACHELLA**

OK, so it's in California but even so, if you get a chance, try it. Imagine a festival conceived by Hollywood screenwriters. Kempt grass, guaranteed sunshine and lots of beautiful and famous people watching legendary bands you thought had split up. That's Coachella. They've had Daft Punk, Madonna, Kanye, LCD Soundsystem and even a performance by a hologram of dead rapper Tupac Shakur.

THE LIFE-CHANGING ONE:
BURNING MAN

Another US entry, Burning Man is 'not a festival'. Organizers say it is a 'grand experiment' and a 'catalyst for creative culture in the world', which takes place in a pop-up city in the Nevada desert. And that is pretty amazing, considering it began in 1986 when a guy named Larry Harvey and some friends hammered together a wooden man (as well as a little wooden dog!) and burned them on a San Francisco beach. The cops said, 'Hey, buddy, what you doin'?' Larry said, 'Please don't shoot! I want to celebrate the solstice!'

Thirty years on, Burning Man is a 'moneyless utopia', founded on ten principles, such as 'radical self-reliance', 'decommodification' and er, 'gifting'. (By our calculation, if you're radically self-reliant and people are gifting stuff to you, you're laughing, right?)

It's hot, it's weird and there's a lot of people dancing and blowing stuff up. Don't worry about your wellies either. Remember, it happens in the desert!

BURNING MAN

THREE FESTIVALS TO DRESS UP AT

BOOMTOWN

BoomTown is conceived as an actual town with a police station, a bank, bars and a leisure centre but the things that happen there redefine civic normality. In fact, the organizers have written an entire story relating how their town was founded by explorer Nickolas Boom and has since battled dark forces. It reads like a screenplay and the place feels like a film set. The bands aren't major rock or indie headliners but the point is the stunning sets and staging.

SECRET GARDEN PARTY

SGP is the brainchild of a man called Freddie Fellowes who threw a 'work party' for 800 events managers in 2003 and decided to do it again the next year as a festival. Things happen in yurts and tree houses set near a lake. There has been pig-racing, effigy-burning, mud wrestling, astronaut training, a mermaid school and an ass-trologer (which, in case you didn't know, is someone who can tell your future by looking at your backside). Bonkers.

Getting to bloody Abbots Ripton in Cambridgeshire can be a bit of a bummer but it isn't called 'secret' for nothing. And the audience participation element is fantastic. In the past, there have been events and competitions organized all weekend specifically for people named Dave. The eventual winner was crowned King of the Daves. People laughed till they cried, even those called Sharon or Keith.

BESTIVAL

Bestival is the acknowledged closer of the festival season. It happens on the Isle of Wight in September (at Robin Hill Country Park, not the same place as the IOW Festival) and though it won consecutive awards as a medium-sized festival, it's now a proper, award-winning big one. Why? Well, how about entering *Guinness World Records* for the largest gathering of people in fancy dress? Or the inflatable church where people can get married?

There is a lot of competition for novel ideas amongst the smaller boutique festivals. Bestival has led the way. Watching Ken Fox's Wall of Death is a very popular hangover cure (a man called Ken whizzes around a vertical wall on a motorbike. The kind and mature part of you wants him to survive. An insane, still-drunk part of you wants him to drop off). Afternoons browsing in the, er, cardboard record shop are also highly recommended.

FESTIVAL
FASHION

FESTIVAL FASHION (WOMEN)

You may think, I am going to a festival. I will therefore wear clean knickers, wellies and a Gore-Tex jacket, and let that be an end to it. But those are 'factory settings' fashion ideas. It is not enough simply to remain clean and dry. You need to make a statement.

Of course, there are no hard and fast rules but it's generally the men who dress up as bears, children's TV characters or pantomime horses at festivals. No reason why you shouldn't, of course, but the novelty outfits are more often associated with young men seeking attention/peacocking.

For the female of the species there is a plethora of more sophisticated styles and looks.

1   Florals and psychedelic colours, smocks and sandals. 'Hippy' is the classic festival look, a tribute to the original flower-power generation.

2   With off-the-shoulder blouses and big earrings, the boho look shares much with the hippy but be warned: strangers may expect you to be able to read palms or predict their futures.

3   You are to be envied if you can carry off leather trousers and mirrored aviators for a more rock/grunge style. It's only recommended for those who can seek refuge in a luxury yurt when it's too hot or raining.

4   It is easy to dress like a raver. You'll need shorts and a T-shirt, a glow stick and a whistle. Shake the stick. Blow the whistle. Arrange your features in an expression of ecstatic pleasure, as though someone has given you a wonderful Christmas present.

5   'Ordinary person at a festival'. Yes, this is a look. If you're coming straight from your exams or from your workplace, then you might not have had time to invest in a festival outfit. In this case, you simply adopt the generic person-at-a-festival look. Jeans. T-shirt. Wellies. Face glitter or tribal markings, if you can. Done.

ACCESSORIES

1   Floral headband
2   Dyed armpit hair
3   Glow stick
4   Beads
5   Jester hat
6   Face/body glitter

THIS IS HOW LOVE FEELS.

KYLIE MINOGUE AT BRITISH SUMMER TIME

FEMALE CELEBRITY FESTIVAL-GOERS

ADELE: Long before she blew Glasto away as a headliner, she was a regular festival punter. In her ethnic-print smock with wizard sleeves, she made a tentative effort to fit in. But Adele doesn't have to try too hard. With her general 'I want a drink and a dance and anyone who tries to stop me can f★★★ off!' attitude, she somehow transcends all festival etiquette.

SIENNA MILLER

FLORENCE WELCH

FLORENCE WELCH: The thing about Florence Welch is that she dresses like she's heading to a gathering of free-thinking space cadets every morning. A festival is merely the externalization of what's already in her head. No wonder she aces it with her own boho hippy aesthetic. Brazen bonkers dresses. Lots of costume jewellery. All kinds of baubles in her hair. Brilliant.

MILLIE MACKINTOSH: She often looks like she's heading to a gymkhana, i.e. a bit too smart and clean, with a definite fear of dirt. However, she has one essential hair tip to offer: French braids. An easy, low-maintenance festival strategy.

KATE MOSS: A regular at Glastonbury, who maintains her brand by not trying too hard. Posh wellies for sure (Hunter are *de rigueur*) but with plain cut-off shorts. Maybe a leather jacket. It's the little things, too: she keeps her hair natural and can hold a pint with one hand as though she's actually enjoying it. Curse the A-lister who tentatively holds their drink with two hands, as if to say, 'This glass is made of plastic and has no stem! How does it work? Call my assistant!'

SIENNA MILLER: The actress scores points with a well-judged shawl and hat. She scores bonus points for not wearing sunglasses all the time, which is the preferred celeb defence against peasants. But Sienna was on her phone a lot. Phone a friend occasionally to say, 'I'm by the hog roast!' but taking what looked like a conference call from your agent/director/co-star? Not cool.

ATE MOSS

LILY ALLEN: A regular and reliable festival face, she doesn't deal in fashion clichés. A sundress with wellies or a maxi dress with wellies are just two of her big sartorial risks. Multi-coloured hair is also an area of expertise. Like Adele, her general stance seems to be: 'Look, I'm wearing what I found on the bedroom floor this morning. Is that a problem, sweet cheeks?'

CRESSIDA BONAS: The ex-girlfriend of Prince Harry amazed festival crowds by wearing a pair of cut-off denim dungarees to Glastonbury. Yes, *dungarees*. That's half an hour getting undressed every time you want to go to the toilet.

ALEXA CHUNG: She knows how to pull off a good festival look. The beaded shawl is great for chilly evenings, the cute neckerchief is just, well, cute, and she always accessorizes with plentiful medallions and necklaces to complete the look of a devil-may-care shambling hippy. However, if we're going to be picky she is just too *clean*. An easy celeb mistake to make. Hair glossy and shiny. Wellies box-fresh. Get some mud on you!

EMMA WATSON: At Glastonbury in 2010, a brash and drunk young man was heard to ask the Harry Potter star, 'Don't s'pose you could use your wand to magic me up a lamb kebab? I'm starving.' She couldn't, but apart from that, her festival appearances have been impeccable. Her camouflage-patterned bodice was a particular fashion favourite.

CARA DELEVINGNE: Wellies, cut-off jeans, throwing a peace sign, wearing a baseball cap backwards. Cara makes it look easy.

COLEEN ROONEY: WAGs at festivals ring alarm bells. Their high-maintenance blow-drys do not fare well in testing rock 'n' roll conditions. However, there is one exception: Coleen Rooney. Coleen likes a drink and she likes a festival. Her festival style is 'home counties mum walking the dogs' but that's OK.

FESTIVAL FASHION (MEN)

There are complex socio-cultural reasons – which we won't explore here – explaining why it is much easier for men to dress for festivals. But take it from us: it is much easier for men to dress at festivals. Men can wear anything. Shorts. Jeans and a T-shirt. However, if you want to attract attention/get hugs, then you might consider the following:

1   A onesie. Cute is best. A bear or a puppy. This outfit says, 'Feel free to approach me. I share many of the qualities embodied by the animal I am impersonating!'

2   A Viking outfit. You can hire them, complete with horned helmet, faux-fur belted jerkin and sword. This gives the signal that you have come to 'pillage, plunder and lay waste', albeit ironically.

3   Women's clothing. A wig, mini-skirt and heels. Done classy, this says: 'I am comfortable exploring my sexuality and challenging gender stereotypes.' But if you ham it up too much, it will say: 'I'm on a stag do and this is all very ironic but actually I am terrified of the transgender issue in all its manifestations.'

4   Tweed and a jacket. Ironically rising above it all and looking like you are on a pheasant shoot but have stumbled into the wrong field/century.

MALE CELEBRITY FESTIVAL-GOERS

BRADLEY COOPER: The Hollywood heart-throb has been spotted at Coachella and Glasto. A grubby T-shirt and a waxy rainproof Barbour jacket are perfect. His outfit says: 'Look, I know I haven't got the proper kit and I'm a bit too old for this malarkey but someone gave me a ticket and I just really wanted to be here, OK?'

LOUIS TOMLINSON: The One Direction star is a regular attendee. He scores points for reaching out to the rock community, where cheesy, talent-contest popstars are not always welcome. But he gets marked down severely for wearing pristine, white tennis shoes and being accompanied by a gopher who carries his bags.

NICK GRIMSHAW: Sometimes when you spot a radio 'broadcaster' at a festival there is a distinct sense they'd rather be playing CDs back in the warm studio booth with a steaming hot cup of coffee in hand. With Radio One DJ Nick Grimshaw, it's the opposite; he's like a wild animal that's been returned to live in its natural habitat. He wears ripped jeans and beads. He lets his signature quiff droop like a collapsed two-man tent. Grimshaw has perfected the elegantly wasted look personified.

NICK GRIMSHAW

THERE'S A LOT TO BE
SAID FOR WATCHING
IT ON TELLY.

JARVIS COCKER

FASHION FAQS

HOW LONG CAN I KEEP MY FESTIVAL WRISTBAND ON WITHOUT BECOMING A PUBLIC HYGIENE THREAT OR LOOKING LIKE A DICK?

It's the end of the summer and you are back at uni or work. You want everyone to know that you attended several festivals and so you keep those wristbands on, despite an array of daily hazards. You get food on them. You keep them on. You get printer ink on them. You keep them on. Finally, your granny asks what that ratty bit of material dangling from your arm is when you pass her a Christmas sherry. Ditch it by Christmas.

HOW LONG DO I KEEP MY ACCESS ALL AREAS LAMINATE AROUND MY NECK AFTERWARDS WITHOUT . . . ETC.?

Fine, so you chaperoned a hobbling headliner to the backstage medic that time he broke his leg onstage. You want everyone to know you work in rock so you keep the laminate on. But seriously, it starts to look a bit desperate when you're still wearing it the following spring.

IS IT TRUE EVERYONE SECRETLY HATES THE PERSON WHO BRINGS AN ACOUSTIC GUITAR?

It shouldn't be the case but yes, it is true. The guy or girl who arrives in buckskins, with a guitar strapped to their back, is secretly despised. Sure, it's a musical instrument and you are at a music festival. But it's just annoying. Especially at 3 a.m. Leave 'Wonderwall' to the professionals.

NOTHING WORTHWHILE EVER HAPPENS AFTER 2 A.M. ESPECIALLY IN A FESTIVAL TATTOO PARLOUR. IS THIS TRUE?

Henna is the acceptable festival body art. It's Eastern and spiritual and is the make-up equivalent of saying, 'I think very deeply about alternative cultures and smoke a bit of weed'. Also, it comes off. But getting a proper tattoo at a festival is ill-advised.

HOW CAN I MAKE SURE MY MUM SEES ME ON THE TELLY?

Lots of festivals get filmed for TV or band documentaries, and everyone wants to be included in an amazing panning shot across the crowd. But how can you make sure your face is in it? The hilarious T-shirt or home-made banner is one possibility (see page 69).

THINGS TO BRING (EVERYONE)

1   A tent. If it claims to be a two-man but costs less than £30, then it's probably not a tent, just a refuse sack. Seriously, take a decent one. It should be waterproof. And put it up in the back garden first to make sure all the poles, pegs and guy ropes are there.

2   A camping chair. You may imagine you'll be sitting cross-legged in a circle, toasting marshmallows on the fire, but you won't be. You'll want something off the ground, preferably with a cup holder in the arm.

3   Sleeping bag. Make sure it's a warm one and keep it rolled in a plastic bag. If it gets wet, you will be very sad.

4   A bag with a cross-body strap or, if your self-esteem can take it, a bum bag. You will want to carry money, wet wipes, sun cream, sunglasses and your phone. Alternatively, wear trousers with very baggy pockets.

5   A hat. Few festivals have any natural shade. If you are lucky enough and the sun is shining, something with a brim will be very useful. Also the perfect cover-up for bad-hair days.

6   Plenty of underwear and socks. A clean, dry set of these essentials can provide the feel-good equivalent of a spa weekend.

7   Layers. It's all about adapting to changing temperatures. Vest, shirt, fleece, coat, etc. And remember, cloudless summer days = freezing-cold nights. Bring a jumper to sleep in.

8   Wellies/Converses. Relax your need to make a fashion statement with these. Take cheapo options and, in the case of Converses, be prepared for them to get destroyed/lost.

9   Sunglasses.

10   Spare bin liners. There is no launderette at your festival. Keep wet and dirty clothes safely away from your precious clean ones. In the bag they go! Destination? Mum and dad's laundry basket!

11   Wash bag. You thought you'd just rough it for four days? Don't. You will have so much more fun if you maintain basic hygiene. Bring some shower gel, a toothbrush, toothpaste and deodorant. At the very least, take wet wipes.

12   First-aid kit. Plasters for blisters, Imodium, Berocca, Nurofen, Dioralyte, sun cream, hand sanitizer – the essentials.

13   Torch. For when your iPhone runs out of battery.

14   Lighter, bottle/can opener.

15   Two-ring camping stove. (See also Festival Food, page 96.)

16   Phone charger.

17   Take your iPhone if you cannot live without it. But festivals and technology can be a bad mix. Think about leaving it at home and using a cheap pay-as-you-go brick phone.

18   A tenner in your shoe. Seriously, an emergency tenner can be the difference between making an admirably self-reliant recovery and that ridiculous tearful phone call home to mummy.

EXTRA THINGS (FOR HER)

* Eye mask
* Ear plugs
* Glitter
* Dry shampoo
* Floral headband
* Fake tan
* Nail varnish
* Tampons
* Hair ties
* Hair clips
* Spare sunglasses
* A couple of necklaces
* A collection of rings
* Your make-up bag: OK, so obviously you are not going for the cover-girl look. However, when you catch your reflection in a big muddy puddle, you want to look good, right? Swap your normal classy eye-shadow tones for something neon or Day-Glo. Don't forget tweezers, concealer and waterproof mascara.

EXTRA THINGS (FOR HIM)

* Beard trimmer

Plaits used to be the look associated with young Swiss girls living as part of isolated cheese-making families or perhaps a desolate queen moping around Hampton Court waiting to be beheaded. But then came festivals, and plaits are now totally back in fashion. Without a hairbrush (you lost it while singing into it during drunken karaoke) or shampoo (you were hungry and spread it on toast), plaits are the perfect hair disaster-management choice. After days in the mosh pit, effectively sleeping rough, you will need an easy-care option. Go for loose plaits and pin them away from your face to keep yourself cool in the sun.

ONLY BRITISH PEOPLE WOULD DANCE AND SING IN THE RAIN AND I THINK THAT'S KINDA BEAUTIFUL.

STEVIE WONDER

FLAGS

Whether it's 'Give Peace a Chance' or 'Wayne loves Becky', you *must* wave a flag. Failing that, an inflatable piece of fruit. Those legendary photos of festival crowds holding things aloft don't organize themselves, you know. Get involved! And a flag is invaluable for telling friends and family where you are.

Things to wave in ascending order of madness:

1   Inflatable banana. Zany, yes. Childish? That too. Inflatable bananas have been a festival and football-match staple for years now. After ten pints they retain a certain louche suggestiveness but they are beginning to look like the 'can't be bothered' choice of the lazy.

2   A pirate flag. Indicative of rebelliousness. Fine in the 1970s but now that they sell them in Ikea? No.

3   An inflatable globe. Yes, it indicates that we share this planet and a common humanity. Bit cheesy but OK.

4   Xylobands. The flashing wristbands that Coldplay first gave out during their 2012 Mylo Xyloto tour. Yes, it's cool that you have one. But, and it's a big but, they only flash when Coldplay's Head of Flashing Lights programmes them to.

Try displaying these slogans on a prominent T-shirt or flag:

1   'It's hammered time!' A jaunty play on rapper MC Hammer's catchphrase, this was first spotted at Reading in the 1990s.

2   'What do we want? A cure for Tourette's. When do we want it? C★★★.'

3   'Atheism: a non-prophet organization.'

4   'ANGB: it's bang out of order.'

5   'Trust in science: alcohol is a solution.'

6   The name of your hometown.

FINALLY MEETING MY PORTALOO

SOME OF THE WEIRD THINGS THAT HAVE HAPPENED AT FESTIVALS

'I got married at Glastonbury!'

We got married a couple of weeks before Glastonbury and our friends organized a handfasting blessing ceremony for us at the festival. It was so much fun. We had hen and stag parties the night before, coupled with a veil, top hats, and hen and stag festival wristbands! The ceremony was held in the Healing Fields by a priestess called Glenda. We had to tie ribbons round our hands (a Celtic tradition to 'tie the knot'), share cake and ale with our guests, and the blessing ended with us jumping over a big broom. It was beautiful and just like having a second wedding day with vows and readings, only this time in wellies and a simple dress.

Unfortunately, it rained – as is expected at Glastonbury – but it didn't dampen our spirits and we went on to celebrate some more in the mud afterwards. It was the perfect way to celebrate our wedding and a magical memory we will treasure for ever!

SIAN THOMAS, LIVERPOOL

'I had a baby at a festival!'

In 2010, thirty-year-old Victoria Iremonger went into labour as soon as she arrived at Glastonbury. She said: 'I wasn't due for another two weeks and so I thought I'd be fine. I was just starting to enjoy myself when my waters broke and I realized the baby was coming. I never expected this to happen but it was a great start to the festival. It really made my weekend.'

In fact, she gave birth in a nearby hospital and then returned to the festival with her new baby Reuben and stayed for the rest of the weekend.

'I got trench foot!'

It was the wettest Glastonbury in years. I was well-prepared but I got a bit drunk and melted a hole in my welly by putting it too near our campfire. The water got in and over the following day my sock and foot got wetter and wetter. Then my foot went cold, then sore, then numb. By Sunday, it looked really odd: yellowy-white, like uncooked chicken past its sell-by date. I went to the medical tent where they diagnosed trench foot. It's serious. Your foot is basically dying and if it gets infected, it has to be amputated. I dried it out and warmed it but it took weeks to get fully better.

GUY MARSHALL, LONDON

'I fell in the chemical toilets!'

In 2009, eighteen-year-old Charlotte Taylor from Sunderland spent 20 minutes with her head and shoulders wedged in a chemical toilet at Leeds Festival.

'As I got up to leave [the toilet], I swung my body round to open the door and my handbag slipped off my arm and disappeared down the toilet. It had my phone, ticket and all my money in, so if I left it I would have been stranded. I put one hand down but I couldn't reach so I put the other one down to try and grab it … I was straining so far down that I got wedged. My shoulders were stuck on both sides and I couldn't move at all. I kept saying to myself, "Oh my God, I can't believe this is happening, it can't be real." '

Festival fire fighters were eventually called to the scene and managed to pull Charlotte free. She was hosed down and bravely opted to continue with her weekend.

'Throughout the rest of the festival I could hear people talking about it,' she continues. 'The rumours got out of control. I heard one that a dwarf had fallen in and drowned.'

'I found strangers sleeping in my tent!'

I was at WOMAD in 2015 and had brought along a roomy three-person tent for me and my boyfriend, plus all our clothes and cooking gear. We enjoyed the Saturday-night headliners and got back late. But when I pulled down the zipper, I could see two pairs of feet and I could hear snoring. These two girls had crawled into our tent and fallen into a deep, drunken sleep. I couldn't wake them up. They were totally out of it. It was almost dawn, so me and my boyfriend went for a walk to decide what to do. After an hour, we went back to the tent and decided to make breakfast. The noise and smells woke them up and they were pretty apologetic. They said they had got lost. I think of myself as quite liberal and relaxed but when one of them asked if she could have a sausage, I drew the line and I said no.

MARTHA STATHAM, BRISTOL

'I was attacked by a cow!'

I was at Green Man, which takes place in a beautiful part of Wales. After a row with my boyfriend I began to feel a bit claustrophobic, so a friend and I decided to jump the fence and go for a walk in the surrounding fields. I can see it's a bit weird but we felt like we were being rebels. We decided to head to a local village and enjoy a cup of tea and a scone. We stomped across a beautiful field, feeling very free and hippy-like. That's when the cows attacked. It felt like they were angry that these festival-goers had not only invaded their farmland but now also wanted to walk across their field. Cows are scary. They mobbed us and we had to run to get away from them. Festivals put you in the mood of rustic romanticism but livestock aren't necessarily on the same page.

EMILY THWAITE, SHREWSBURY

WHERE DO THE
COWS GO? DO THEY
GET SENT ON A
VACATION?

JAY Z

FESTIVAL RUMOURS

Like Christmas, pre-festival excitement is just as important as the event itself. It begins with the rumours. Shortly after you book your ticket, you will hear that Guns N' Roses are headlining your festival (it always used to be Prince but for obvious reasons he no longer features). Or you might hear that Radiohead are doing a secret gig in a tiny tent. In 2011, this rumour spread round Glastonbury for the fourteenth consecutive year and ... actually turned out to be true.

However, once you are actually on-site amongst a large crowd where word of mouth is at a premium, things become more intense. More extreme and, indeed, utterly insane items of gossip will begin to circulate.

Here are the top five festival rumours:

1 'OH MY GOD, THE QUEEN IS DEAD!'

Sitting around a gas-fired stove during a rain storm at Reading Festival in 1988, two festival-goers discussed their favourite album by indie legends The Smiths, who had recently split up. Their 1986 album *The Queen Is Dead* was mentioned thus: 'Oh my God, *The Queen Is Dead*! Without a shadow of a doubt!' This innocent private conversation promptly burgeoned into a festival-wide rumour of the British monarch's demise.

2 'OH MY GOD, RUSSIA HAS INVADED POLAND!'

Generally considered to be mischief-making by a bored rock fan, this rumour spread at V Festival in 2014. At any large festival, there is always one major geo-political rumour doing the rounds. See also the 2012 T in the Park rumour that North Korea had launched a nuclear attack on London. For reasons best known to the Scots, this was actually met with a cheer and the celebratory clanking together of super-strength lager cans.

3 'GLASTONBURY IS MOVING!'

This rumour began in 2015 and may have some basis in fact. The nearby stately home of Longleat, home to the Marquess of Bath, is the rumoured new venue. However, it would only be for one year, probably in 2019, to give Eavis's farm and the cows a year off.

4 'CLIFF RICHARD IS DEAD!'

The elderly 'British Elvis' Cliff Richard became famous in the sixties. During the 1980s, someone at Glastonbury announced he had died. It wasn't true but it is now traditional for someone at the festival to announce Cliff has kicked the bucket. However, there are more modish variants. 'Jay Z got shot!' is one. 'Pete Doherty is dead!' is another. Or try 'Oh my God, Pete Doherty is alive!' for ironic kudos.

5 'PRINCE HARRY IS IN THE DANCE TENT!'

There are often rumours of a Royal attending a festival. Princesses Beatrice or Eugenie are common faux sightings. That is, until someone realizes it was just a horse in a field baring its gums while eating an apple. Royal-sighting rumours are always false except for when they were uttered at WOMAD in 2013. Because the ginger chap in a trilby, dancing with a burly security guy, really *was* Prince Harry.

WHAT DOES YOUR
FARM LOOK LIKE
WHEN EVERYONE
HAS GONE HOME?
I IMAGINE IT'S
QUITE NICE.

THE QUEEN TO MICHAEL EAVIS
AFTER PRESENTING HIM WITH A
CBE FOR SERVICES TO MUSIC

'MEDIC!'

There have been births and deaths at festivals. Here are the top five situations reported at a festival medical tent:

1   HYPOTHERMIA AND SUNSTROKE

Many festivals offer little shelter from the elements, so when it rains you're going to get cold and wet, and when the sun shines you're going to burn. Even if the daytime weather is fantastic, it may be freezing at night, so take something very warm to sleep in. And getting drunk and falling asleep in the sun without sun cream is madness.

2   TRENCH FOOT

Make sure you have a solid pair of wellies. If you walk around with wet feet for too long, you run the risk of developing trench foot. Your foot gets cold and numb, blood circulation fails and your foot dies!

3   DEHYDRATION

Drinking a lot of alcohol, dancing like a loony and even just walking miles round a large festival all require you to keep well hydrated. Carry a water bottle with you. Sip and survive!

4   DIARRHOEA

I know, I know, they didn't have hand sanitizer at Woodstock. But still, we know a lot more about poo-borne infections than we did in the sixties. You really don't want to get a bug that will ruin your weekend. Clean your hands and use wet wipes after you use the chemical loos.

5 BURNS

People who are tired, drunk, or both are often not the best ones to operate gas camping stoves. Each year someone at a festival will catch fire. Don't be that person.

TIPS AND TRICKS

FESTIVAL HACKS

That petrol looks very expensive – how do I get there for free?

In the good old days (ask a funky granny), you could stand at the side of the road in flared jeans and a cheesecloth shirt, and stick your thumb in the air at passing cars to hitchhike. These days, things are far more organized. Try lift-share sites like GoCarShare (gocarshare.com), which will match you with people offering or looking for lifts.

That fence looks too high – how do I get in for free?

Once upon a time you could climb over the fence. Now, in return for work behind the bar or as a steward, you can receive a free ticket. Bear in mind that the big festivals start hiring five or six months in advance, while smaller ones still need people a few weeks ahead of gates opening.

You might be in charge of attaching wristbands, traffic management, or general stewarding. Some organizations like Oxfam require a deposit, which they will return once you have done your agreed shift(s).

You can apply to Festaff (festaff.co.uk) for work at T in the Park, CTM (Cash & Traffic Management; ctm.uk.com) for Cornbury and Picnic in the Park, and Hotbox (hotboxevents.com) for opportunities at Latitude and Reading & Leeds.

These clothes are sodden/destroyed – how do I survive?

Take good-quality bin liners to the festival (not those see-through, molecule-thin ones from Poundland). If it rains, these bin liners will be not only your friend but your house, and possibly even your outfit.

I lost my friend while having my stomach pumped by a sweet boy from the St John Ambulance – how do I find her?

Download the free app Find My Friends [iOS and Android]. Alternatively, you could establish an emergency meeting point on arrival.

It's dark and I'm drunk – how do I find my tent?

Download the Tent Finder app when you arrive and enter map coordinates once your tent is erected. The app will guide you back with an easy-to-use map.

It's very noisy here – how do I avoid going deaf?

There is no shame in wearing ear plugs. The organization Action On Hearing Loss estimates sound levels near the speakers can reach 110dB – the equivalent of standing next to an operational pneumatic drill.

My inflatable mattress has sprung a leak – how do I get a comfy night's sleep?

Pack a bicycle puncture-repair kit before you go. They are invaluable for fixing mattress leaks and even tent punctures. One regular punter at Reading offers a puncture-repair service. He will come and do mattresses, tents or plastic water storage bags and even offers a 24-hour guarantee for each fix. He charges, literally, £2 a pop.

'THEY SMASHED IT!' A BLUFFER'S GUIDE TO LEGENDARY FESTIVAL PERFORMANCES

Don't shout a rash and ill-informed, 'That was brilliant!' after watching Kaiser Chiefs stumble through a lunchtime set in front of three people. Show knowledge. Evince discernment. Always make reference to the greatest festival performances ever. Just add '... but obviously not as good as Radiohead at Glasto in ninety-seven'.

Depending on how old you are, you can also try referencing:

✳   The Smiths at Glastonbury in 1984.

✳   The original Oasis line-up rocking Glastonbury in 1994.

✳   The Arctic Monkeys at Reading in 2005. Yes, a whole five months before their debut album was released, it was clear they were destined for greatness.

✳   Δ [spoken as Alt-J] at Latitude in 2015. Described as a perfect performance and quickly assuming modern legendary status.

✳   If you are over the age of sixty or very bold, you can try citing Jimi Hendrix at Woodstock. Due to weather and tech problems he didn't get to play until 8.30 a.m. on the Monday morning. He downed a bottle of Blue Nun and played for two hours, even though 90 per cent of the crowd had gone home. It remains one of the all-time legendary festival performances.

ARCTIC MONKEYS AT READING 2005

HOW TO ACHIEVE FESTIVAL IMMORTALITY

Yes, of course, you came to hear some great music and spend time with your friends. But there's always an element of competition, right? Everyone wants to feature in those 'Oh. My. God. What about the time ...' festival war stories.

You will earn immortality for the following:

✳ MAXIMUM POINTS

Being air-lifted to hospital. Any reason will do but bonus points will be awarded for swan-diving off the speaker stack or complete emotional exhaustion.

The following medals will also be made available:

✳ FAIRLY AWESOME

Sleeping while stretched out full-length in the middle of the mosh pit.

✳ QUITE COOL

Having a backstage pass but giving it away to stay with 'the people'.

✳ NOT SO COOL

Having a backstage pass and sneaking in for three-course meals, showers and toilets but otherwise remaining with 'the people'.

✳ TOTALLY UNACCEPTABLE

Booking into a B&B or going home.

I WANT TO FEEL
LIKE THIS EVERY
F***ING DAY
OF MY LIFE.

DAVE GROHL

AMAZING FESTIVAL FOOD

This book is not your mother. Nevertheless, you *must* eat. Subsisting on food from festival stalls will either cost you a fortune or might lead to many wasted hours on a chemical toilet (yeah, we're looking at *your* spicy food, Mexico!). So think about taking as many of these staples as you can:

* **BEEF JERKY** or **CHORIZO** are good meats to take. They have a long shelf-life and will survive without refrigeration (but keep them in a cool place).

* Take **COCONUT MILK** in a ring-pull can as a substitute for cow's milk. Again, it doesn't require refrigeration and you can use it on cereal or even as the base for a curry or a smoothie.

* **BANANAS**. Either fresh or dried from a health-food shop. Extremely nutritious and good for hangovers due to their high potassium content.

* **NUTS**. High in protein and non-perishable.

* **KENDAL MINT CAKE**. A high-energy staple for walkers but great for rock fans too.

* **SUPER NOODLES** and just-add-hot-water oat pots are simple and nutritious snacks.

NB: Seriously, make sure every can you take has a ring pull. Don't be the drunken moron trying to bite or smash into their tin of beans with a rock.

There is a guy at BoomTown who boils and sells eggs. They are a highly nutritious snack and this man was hard-boiling hundreds of the things and selling them for 50p each. Even if you eat nothing else, you can hard-boil a dozen yourself beforehand and take them with you. Store in a cool place and hey presto! Nutrition!

However, if you are a bit more, you know, *classy*, and cosmopolitan street food doesn't intimidate, then consider this. It's obviously quite cool to show knowledge of the different bands at a festival. But in recent years, festival food has changed beyond all recognition and it looks *very* cool when you saunter up to a food stall and show your mates you know what Tibetan momo dumplings look like.

Astound your friends with the following festival eats:

GOAN FISH CURRY

Two syllables, yes? Go-*an,* as in from Goa in India, where your parents had a short-lived hippy phase in the nineties before becoming chartered accountants. It's spicy and healthy. An excellent antidote to the deluge of cheap lager and Pringles.

TIBETAN MOMO DUMPLINGS

OMG, you have to try these! Momos are simple dumplings, which are steamed or fried. Inside, you will find either meat, vegetables or cheese. So far, this is just a very tasty Nepalese street-food snack. But dip it in the accompanying sauce and ... AMAZING!

EMPANADA

This is essentially a pasty but from South America and filled with meat and/or vegetables – sometimes even fruit. You want to sound funky and cosmopolitan, right? If you buy a pasty at the petrol station en route and unwrap it at the festival, it becomes an 'empanada', OK?

HALO-HALO

This is not a meal but a drink from the Philippines. If you are lucky enough to get too hot at a festival or need a pick-me-up after a heavy night, this is perfect. It contains coconut milk, syrup, fruit and mashed red beans. Thus far it's like a milkshake but then it gets crowned with ice-cream or evaporated milk.

BÁNH MÌ

This snack is from Vietnam but if you say it wrong it sounds like you're asking to be thrown out of the festival. Not 'Ban me, please!' but a short, clipped 'Bánh *mì*, please' will bring results. It's a grilled baguette filled with pâté, meatballs or pork and then herbs, mayo and chilli sauce. A South-east Asian backpacker staple and, more recently, a festival favourite.

I LEARNED
SOMETHING
BEAUTIFUL AT
MY FIRST BRITISH
FESTIVAL.
IT DOESN'T
MATTER HOW
BAD YOU SMELL.
YOU JUST HAVE
TO LET IT GO.

BEYONCÉ

TROUBLESHOOTING – WHAT HAPPENS IF . . .?

. . . all the best tent pitches are taken?

So, you rock up at your festival on Saturday afternoon because the weather looked a bit dicey on Friday and you didn't want to compromise your hair or get your new Topshop suede booties wet but . . . oh, no! No one in the vast crowd thought to save you a perfectly level pitch by the lake near the water tap, overlooking the bucolic splendour of the countryside! He*lloooo*, festivals might nominally be about peace, love and understanding, but securing the best camping spot means war. Organize an advanced party who will arrive early, establish a good spot and put up *all* the tents. Yes, they will need to be rewarded but it will be worth it.

If you are left with the last skanky pitches you can still make wise choices. If you don't want to be woken up at 3 a.m. by students playing the bongos or indulging in drinking games, head for Family Camping. There is usually a curfew. Also, never camp near the Portaloos if you can help it. Sure, it's convenient but they smell and also, in a row of twenty or more, the endless rhythm of the self-closing door slamming will drive you nuts.

. . . I lose contact with my friends?

Let's face it, some friends are vague and flaky. When it comes to arranging a meeting at a designated point in the space-time continuum, 'herding kittens into a sack' doesn't really cover it.

'What's your problem? I said the dance tent at twelve!' they squeal. Red as a beetroot with fury, you try to explain there are four dance tents and two different twelve o'clocks every day.

Using an easily recognizable flag is an simple way of finding friends and being found. There's also the Find My Friends app (see page 90). Yes, it's a bit Orwellian but then again, as we've said, some friends are vague and flaky.

. . . I suffer an attack by festival zombies after arranging a supermarket delivery to my tent.

Though you like going to festivals, you don't see why you should forgo the finer things in life. But this is a mistake. Forget your home comforts. At a festival, there is nobility in suffering. Besides, by day three of a festival, people may attack if they see you have fresh on-the-vine tomatoes or toilet paper.

. . . a man in a fluorescent jacket, holding a walkie-talkie, tells me to pour my twelve-pack of beer into a ditch.

Do not pack many cans of beer unless you are sure you a) can bring them in and b) know where you are camping. Some festivals like Glastonbury don't have restrictions on bringing alcohol in while others have deals with major alcohol companies which mean yours will be confiscated.

. . . I fall off my best friend's shoulders while waving at Florence and the Machine.

Encourage your best friend to work out those neck and shoulder muscles during a rigorous six-week training period before your festival. Why? You *will* want to sit on someone's shoulders if you want any chance of actually seeing the headline act. It's important the burden-carrier can act casual while holding you aloft for at least three songs. Staggering about under your weight is unacceptable. Dropping you is a relationship-ender.

FESTIVAL
FACTS

ARE THERE ANY WINTER FESTIVALS?

You haven't had enough festival fun in the summer? Yes, there are some off-season specials available but you'll have to travel.

Rise Festival in Les Deux Alpes in France happens mid-December. It's actually a 'ski and party' affair. You go on the piste during the day and then rock out at night. Eurosonic Noorderslag in Groningen, Holland occurs in mid-January. Don't expect big names because you won't find them, but if you're interested in new bands playing in a beautiful ancient city then this is a hidden gem. Where's the Music? happens mid-February in Norrköping, Sweden. Again, no big names and the onus is on home-grown talent.

WHAT DOES A HEADLINE BAND GET PAID FOR AN APPEARANCE?

Jimi Hendrix got paid £30k for two performances at Woodstock. The Rolling Stones asked for £16 million to play the 2016 Coachella festival. Top acts routinely ask for £1 million for the commercial festivals like V or Wireless. However, because Glastonbury is for charity, Coldplay and McCartney both did it for £200,000 each. Acts way down the bill often get nothing.

WHAT DO PERFORMERS HAVE ON THEIR BACKSTAGE 'RIDER'?

Before he plays a show Iggy Pop issues an eighteen-page document of backstage requests. One item he demanded on a 2006 rider is 'a copy of *USA Today* that's got a story about morbidly obese people in it'. It also states that Iggy doesn't want a 'typical rock 'n' roll dressing room' and goes on to suggest to promoters: 'Just let someone loose with a little bit of artistic flair. Er, do you know any homosexuals?'

I HEARD A MAJOR FESTIVAL WAS ALMOST CANCELLED DUE TO TWO MATING BIRDS. TRUE?

True. In 2015, T in the Park was almost cancelled because two rare ospreys began nesting at the venue. It is illegal to disturb protected species when they are mating. Although alternative nesting arrangements were offered, the birds ignored them. Finally, after £500,000 was spent on an 'osprey mitigation plan', the festival went ahead. Weirdly enough, Noel Gallagher's High Flying Birds headlined.

WOODSTOCK ORGANIZERS wanted John Lennon to appear but US president Nixon didn't want him in the country because he was considered a national security threat.

JIMI HENDRIX and his band drank a bottle of Blue Nun before going on stage at Woodstock.

IT'S A SHIT SHOW.

WOODSTOCK LOCAL
INTERVIEWED BY ABC NEWS
IN 1969

IT TAKES SIX WEEKS to clear up after Glastonbury festival. Eighteen hundred volunteers do the initial rubbish clearance. A priority is to remove stray tent pegs because Michael Eavis's cows have eaten them in the past and died.

YOU COULD START A CHAIN OF CAMPING STORES with the stuff that gets left behind at Glastonbury. In 2015, 6,500 sleeping bags were abandoned. There were also 5,500 tents, 3,500 air beds and 400 gazebos left on the farm.

THE WORLD'S BIGGEST ROCK FESTIVAL is America's Summerfest, held over eleven days in late June/early July each year. *Guinness World Records* has certified attendances of between 800,000 and 1 million rock fans at the event.

HOW MANY PODIATRISTS DOES IT TAKE TO ERADICATE AN OUTBREAK OF FESTIVAL TRENCH FOOT?

Answer: thirteen. That's how many they have at Glastonbury. Trench foot (also known as immersion foot) is caused by lack of blood supply to cold or wet feet and can lead to numbness, sores, gangrene and eventual amputation. Ninety cases a day were reported at the rain-soaked 1998 Glastonbury festival, the worst outbreak since the First World War.

IN 2010, GLASTONBURY FOUNDER Michael Eavis was ranked amongst the 100 most influential people in the world by *Time* magazine. He was placed between Barack Obama and chat-show host Jay Leno.

MICHAEL EAVIS'S LATE WIFE, JEAN, was an 'amateur psychotherapist', who was skilled at calming the pre-show nerves of rock stars.

ARE FESTIVALS ALWAYS SO MALE?
Fifty-four per cent of festival fans are male and 46 per cent are women. However, 82 per cent of artists are male.

THE AVERAGE AGE of a festival headline act in 1995 was thirty years old. By 2015, it was forty-five. Some critics say that it's because festivals have tried to attract an older, wealthier audience because they're now so expensive. For example, a standard weekend ticket to Latitude cost £95 in 2006. In 2015, it cost £190.

IN A 2015 SURVEY, 58 per cent of festival-goers said they went for atmosphere and experience. Only 7 per cent went to see the headline act.

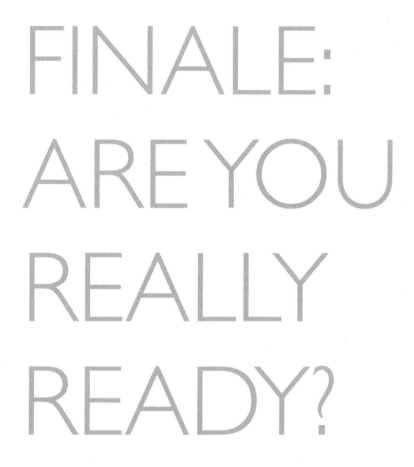

I WILL NOT DO FESTIVALS. THE THOUGHT OF AN AUDIENCE THAT BIG FRIGHTENS THE LIFE OUT OF ME.

ADELE IN 2011

ADELE AT GLASTONBURY
2016

"OH MY GOD,
OH MY GOD,
OH MY GOD.
HI! THIS IS THE
BEST FUCKING
MOMENT OF MY
WHOLE LIFE!"

ADELE HEADLINING AT
GLASTONBURY IN 2016

Have you paid attention to all the useful tips and suggestions in this book? Or have you just been sitting there and laughing at all the pictures of people lying in the mud or dressed up as elves? We hope not. You're not supposed to be enjoying yourselves. This book is all about 'edutainment'.

Let's see just how much you have been paying attention with our 'Are You Really Ready?' quiz.

1 **You have secured a great pitch for you and your friends but a couple of late-arriving strangers cannot find a space for their tent. Do you:**

a Give them a space in your tent circle and offer them a beer to make them feel at home.

b Give them a space just outside the tent circle next to the recycling bins and refuse their offer of a get-to-know-them beer.

c Drive them away like a chimp leading an attack on a rival gang.

2   **There are three incredible acts performing at 10 p.m. on the Saturday night. You need to decide how to resolve this clash of incredible talent. Do you:**

    a   Use the Clashfinder website (clashfinder.com) to analyse which band is going to be most difficult to see over the next few festivals and make your choice accordingly.

    b   Take a punt based on where everyone else seems to be heading.

    c   Have no idea who any of these artists are and spend the evening wandering the campsite asking to borrow a tin opener and wondering why nobody seems to be in?

3   **You have borrowed a tent for the festival from your friend Emma. Emma has just returned from a festival and seems a bit wasted. As she hands the tent bag over to you, she slurs that she thinks 'everything is there'. Do you:**

    a   Say, 'Thanks, Emma' but then put up Emma's tent in the back garden and spend a night in it, expelling all the dead spiders and traces of vomit, and replacing bent tent pegs.

    b   Believe her when she says that 'everything is there'.

    c   You forget to bring a tent. Someone told you that you can buy them on site or you blithely plan to make a new friend who will put you up for the night.

4   You have always wanted to stage-dive because it just looks such awesome fun. Do you:

a   Choose one of the intimate, low stages where you swallow-dive daintily into a thick portion of burly looking guys who have made welcoming eye contact which seems to say, 'It's fine, jump!'

b   Run on to the stage, shut your eyes and leap, hoping for the best.

c   Climb on to the main stage, which has a twenty-foot drop, evade security who give chase and then throw yourself into thousands of pounds worth of gear set up in the photographers' pit below.

5   Everyone knows that it's uncool to expect five-star catering at a rock festival. However, you also know that the human body has basic nutritional needs that must not go unanswered for long periods of time. Do you:

a   Make one meal a day with friends, which will contain at least three of the main food groups.

b   Have a chocolate bar for each day.

c   Decide food is for pussies. You've heard that the ketchup and mustard bottles on a table outside the burger van contain all the nutrients you need.

6   **OK, so a festival is not a military exercise, but actually the US army motto 'Leave no man behind' seems like a good one when you are going to survive in a field full of drunk rock fans with your friends. Do you:**

a   Quietly and unobtrusively take on the role of group leader. You make sure that all your pals make contact at least once a day and when you see them talking to a gaunt-looking man offering to sell them some pills, you intervene and say: 'She's not ill so she doesn't want any of your stupid pills, good*bye*!' and drag her away.

b   If you see a member of your gang, you high-five them but if they go missing, then leave it to the St John Ambulance to sort them out.

c   You don't have any friends.

7   **A Japanese news crew approaches you and asks you why British people enjoy going to festivals so much. Do you:**

a   Say, 'People attend festivals for different reasons. It's partly the music and friendship but also the free-thinking and creative, pan-cultural outlook which sometimes challenges the orthodoxy of living in a Western capitalist society.'

b   Say, 'I want to see Rihanna because I fancy her.'

c   Say, 'I don't know why I am here and now that it is raining I am wondering if I can get my money back, because no one told me the British countryside doesn't have a roof.'

8   **On the very first night, the heavens open and it begins to pour with rain. Do you:**

a   Shrug, put on wellies, pull a bin bag over your head and tell yourself the rain is all part of the amazing tapestry of rural life.

b   Cry.

c   Angrily search for the Customer Services desk and make threats about suing the organizers.

9   **You hear a woman crying about her lost wedding ring and then see it glinting in the shit in a Portaloo. Do you:**

    a   Heroically get it out of the sludge and give it back to her.

    b   Exit the Portaloo and tell her where she can retrieve it.

    c   Carry on with your ablutions, ensuring the trinket is lost in the brown stuff for ever.

10 **You spot a rock star enjoying the festival vibe incognito. Do you:**

    a   Say, 'Hi, I enjoyed your last album and look forward to seeing you on the main stage later' and move on quickly.

    b   Shriek in recognition and ask for his/her autograph.

    c   Follow him/her and ring a tabloid newspaper, offering to report everything that he/she does.

ANSWERS

MOSTLY As: Well done. You are mentally and physically prepared for a rock festival. You embody the spirit of festivals and are a credit to their positive collective ideals.

MOSTLY Bs: You are a borderline case. You know what the right thing to do is, but sometimes you just can't help being a bit of a dick.

MOSTLY Cs: You are not a very accomplished festival-goer. It's hard to determine exactly what it is but here are some pointers: you are selfish and immature and not ready to understand that festivals are about thousands of people bonding and sharing and living together as one in a tent utopia. You might want to try attending some alternative outdoor gatherings, like stock-car racing or dog-fighting, for example.

"IF I HAVE ANY MONEY
SPARE IT'LL GO ON
A NEW SLURRY PIT,
NOT A SWIMMING
POOL OR A HOLIDAY
IN BARBADOS."

MICHAEL EAVIS

Picture Acknowledgements

Every effort has been made to obtain the necessary permissions with reference to copyright material. We apologize for any omissions in this respect and will be pleased to make the appropriate acknowledgements in future editions.

The publisher would like to thank Alamy (page 78), Alice Youell (pages 54, 80 and 114, middle), Charlie Margesson (page 37), Darcy Nicholson (page 16), Hayley Symonds (pages 8, middle, 21, 56, 64, 69 and 72), Rosie Margesson (pages 8, top, 94–5, 105 and 109), Kyla Dean (pages 8, bottom and 86, middle), PA Images (pages 6-7, 10, 12, 13, 17, 20, 24, 34, 38, 40, top, 42, 48, left and right, 52-3, 59, 60, 77, 85, 91, 96, 102-3, 116, 119 and 124), Shutterstock (pages 14, 18, middle and bottom, 40, middle and bottom, 43, 46, 57, 62, 63, 64-65, 66, 76, 82, 88, 90, 106, 108, 112, 114, bottom, 121 and 122) and www.timeincukcontent.com (pages 18, top, 22, 23, 25, 26, 29, 31, 32, 36, 39, 45, 48, middle, 50, 68, 70, 74-75, 86, top and bottom, 93, 98, 99, 100, 114, bottom, 118 and 126) for these photographs.